The Magic Show From Hell (2024)

By
Victoria Holland

The Magic Show From Hell (2024)

Copyright © 2024 by Victoria Holland

Printed In United States Of America
Published by : ACH Publishing

DEDICATION

If you've been following me for a long time, you'd know that Papa Grande Di Magico, the antagonist of this series, is a very old original character of mine. He's gone through many changes since his original creation in 2007. I introduced him to the internet in late 2013. I honestly had no idea what I was doing. The online world was so new to my newly teenage self. I was on edge constantly and almost gave up on creation many times thanks to heavy pushback by so-called critics. In the end, I managed to gain the courage to continue thanks to my wonderful friends that I made along the way.

I wouldn't have made it where I am today without any of them and my fans. I wanted to give a special mention to these wonderful people.

Promptus, Danceofangels, Ivydarkrose, Danatheghost, Adir_Zrihan, Creepymaster_chan, Mama-Devil, the_catcake, Depresso_bean, Lilweaklin, Melonisapotato, nikkikirkland, Pumpkin Queen, The Plague Master, Anis Ranya_artwork and MANY more!

Keep on writing, keep on drawing, keep on being amazing. Thank you, for everything.

"Jasper, check this out!" a girl's voice echoed from inside an abandoned house full of scattered books and ancient furniture. It was late at night, and the moon's rays shone through the home's broken windows. A young man, Jasper, moved past various pieces of furniture and towards the female with a slightly curious look on his face.

"Mary, what did you find?" Jasper asked, leaning in to examine what Mary had found. They were both avid explorers of abandoned places. They had seen many curiosities, such as old toys, necklaces, and various references to past media stored in the home. It was like a time machine, and they loved its mystery.

"I found something under the bed. It looks kind of dirty, but it might be worth keeping," Mary replied, lifting a filthy poster rolled up behind a bookshelf. Jasper raised an eyebrow and placed his hands on his hips.

"I know you have a knack for collecting posters, but that seems like it's not exactly sellable," he mumbled. She rolled her eyes and then held it close to herself. She was already covered in grime from how wet the living room floor was in this house.

"Historical significance is always important; the same is true of old-school pop culture. I don't care if it's partially destroyed; it will look so cool in my collection!" Mary boasted. With a sigh, Jasper shook his head and pulled out his phone. The light of it cast a slight glow in the darker room.

"It's getting late. We should head out. I'd rather not face Mom's wrath. We could just come back here tomorrow to do more exploring," Jasper suggested, showing the time on his phone.

"Aw, but I was having so much fun. You're such a party pooper," Mary pouted. Jasper chuckled a bit in response.

"Yeah, I get that a lot, but seriously, I'd rather not get chewed out by my mom." Jasper leaned down and picked up his bag that was on the floor. After all, the two teenagers had been at the house for half of the day.

"Can I at least see the poster before we enter the rain? I want to see what it is before we tuck it in a bag." Mary slowly started to open the poster. Jasper, growing a bit curious, peered over her shoulder. As the poster opened, it was destroyed in several segments, but one thing caught their eye.

"The heck is this?" Jasper asked with an eyebrow lifted. The poster had several faded big text words that appeared bright in the past. It also had a man in the center, but most of his face had water damage.

"Um, I'm honestly having trouble making out the words." Mary mumbled, "Can you make them out?" She asked Jasper, holding the poster towards him. Jasper squinted his eyes.

"Papa Grande's Magic Show...?" Jasper reads, "I hope I'm reading it right. Is this a TV series or...?"

"I don't know, Jasper. It sounds familiar, but I've never really looked into it." Mary glanced over the words and then at the man in the center of the poster.

"Well, there's also some text on the corner. It's pretty faded, but I can read 1993." Jasper points at the corner of the poster.

"1993? Well, I guess I'll maybe look into this?" Mary then heard Jasper's flip phone vibrate. Jasper released a soft groan between his lips and looked at the number texting him.

"Damn it, I need to go. It's mom, and she's pissed. If you look into the history behind that poster, let me know. I need to head home before she drills my head in." Jasper begins to text his mom as he walks towards the exit of the abandoned house. Mary watched him leave and then glanced at the poster before shoving it inside her bag.

"Okay, I'm coming! Hold on! Wait for me, Jasper!" Mary yelled, quickly catching up to her best friend as he exited the house.

"Too slow!" Jasper teased her as he walked through the tall grass surrounding the house. He knocked away some vegetation with his hand and glanced back at Mary. Mary shoved him slightly as she caught up to him.

"Oh yeah? I bet that I can beat you home!" She replied, throwing the bag over her shoulder.

"Is that a challenge?"

"You bet your ass that it is!"

"Challenge accepted, you're on," Jasper said, quickly running through the grass and bushes. Mary gasped and quickly trailed behind him, holding her bag close.

"You didn't say that we were starting!" She shouted. Jasper ignored her and ran ahead, leaving her in the dust. After several minutes of running, the two worn-out teens arrived at a relatively small neighborhood. They stopped near a white house with a black roof. Jasper quickly dashed onto his front porch and turned back to the highly exhausted girl.

"Beat ya!" he told her, smirking. Mary panted, entirely out of breath. Her hand grasped hold of the railing of the steps.

"Yeah, yeah, go ahead and brag some more." She shoved him with her hand slightly, her arm then flopped down. The door to the house opened up and caught their attention fully. Standing at the door, Jasper's mother stared at her son, her mouth pursed, and her brows narrowed.

"Jasper Young, it's about nine in the evening! I've been texting you to come home!" she said, lecturing Jasper. Jasper's brows curved upwards, and his cheeks shifted to gain a red hue.

"Mom, please, not in front of Mary. This is embarrassing-"

"Mary's parents are worried too. You have never been out this late without letting me know where you're going! You both need to be more responsible!" Mrs. Young scolded the two teens.

Jasper only groaned. Mary sighed and lowered her head a bit. "That's an oopsie on our part. We'll try to be more responsible, I promise!" Mary told Mrs. Young with her hands clasped together.

"Sorry, Mom..." Jasper sighed. Mrs. Young pinched between her eyebrows.

"Just please, try to get better at being more responsible. I don't want either of you to get in trouble. Now, where were you two?" Mrs. Young demanded.

"We went to that abandoned house a couple of miles away. The Victorian-like one with the black shutters and white chipped paint." Mary replied, her whole body tensing up a bit. "It's also my fault. I grabbed Jasper at the last minute after school. Don't get mad at him, I just-"

"Okay, so, did you two take anything? You know that the county owns private property, right?" Mrs. Young told them. "If anyone caught you, you could have been brought back by the police or even be fined."

"Well, we only took a poster, but that's it! I promise!" Mary said, holding her bag close to her side. Mrs. Young shook her head slowly.

"I don't want to see either of you get in trouble. A poster shouldn't do much harm, but..."

"Would you like to see it?" Mary interrupted, beginning to unzip the bag. Mrs. Young gazed at Mary as she slowly pulled out the old poster. As Mary straightened it out and held it out towards Mrs. Young, Mrs. Young's mouth dropped, and she looked away from the poster. Jasper quickly took notice of this.

"Mom?" Jasper said, "Is everything alright?"

"Yeah, it's just... I recommend throwing that poster away. It's an interesting find, but a dark one." Mrs. Young replied, keeping her eyes away from the poster.

Mary, growing more curious, took another glance at the poster.

"Um, do you know more about what it is?" Mary asked. Mrs. Young's brows furrowed even more.

"Yes, but I won't talk about it in detail. The man on that poster did something horrible. It traumatized many of us who were present back in 1993. That's all that I will say," Mrs. Young explained, then crossed her arms again.

"You should go home now and get rid of the poster while you're at it. The history of that man is best forgotten," Mrs. Young concluded, then left to go to her bedroom. Jasper could hear Mary emitting a soft chuckle. He knew very well that she wouldn't get rid of it; if anything, his mother piqued her interest.

"Well, I'm going to head home now. I should keep the poster hidden from my parents too, huh?" Mary whispered to Jasper.

"Yeah, I would. Are you going to look up more on this, I'm assuming?" Jasper asked.

"Hell yeah, I have to now. Want me to text you about what I find?" Mary said while walking towards the door.

"Yeah, go ahead. I'd be lying if I said Mom's freak out didn't pique my interest a little, too," Jasper whispered while watching her leave. After Mary left the home, Jasper retired to his bedroom for the night.

As night came and went, the sound of doves stirred Jasper awake from under his sheets. His tired eyes slowly opened, and he glanced at his alarm clock. It was nine in the morning, which was relatively early for this teenager to snap awake. The sound of early morning cartoons in the background with their wacky hijinks made him more aware.

"Jasper!" Mrs. Young's voice echoed from downstairs. His body jolted upwards a bit, startled.

"What?! I just woke up!" Jasper yelled back. Footsteps were heard coming up his stairs, followed by the door opening, revealing an eleven-year-old girl.

"I'm going to work again! I'll be back tonight! Can you watch over Rose for me?" Mrs. Young asked. Jasper rolled his eyes, and Rose rolled her own.

"Mom! I'm eleven years old! I don't need Jasper to watch over me!" She stomped a foot in anger.

"I don't want to hear it from you two. You both are siblings, have some bonding time or something! I'll be back!" With that, the door slammed shut, leaving the two siblings alone.

Rose looked out the window as Mrs. Young's vehicle pulled out of their driveway and drove off. Her lips curved into a grin.

"Jasper, I'm hungry."

"And...?"

"Make me something? Please, maybe some Mac and Cheese?"

"Make it yourself."

"Jasper! I'm-"

"Eleven years old, and you don't need a babysitter after all, so get to it." The siblings started bickering back and forth, ending with Rose crossing her arms with a frustrated look. As she locked her gaze on Jasper for several seconds, Jasper lifted a brow, becoming unsettled.

"Okay, if I help you make that god-awful breakfast idea, please stop staring at me like that."

"With a peeled orange?"

"Yeah, but that's a bonus to leave me alone for a while, okay?" Jasper grabbed Rose's head and messed her hair up as he left his room. He pulled his phone from his pocket and checked the various messages, seeing many from Mary.

"Agh, crap. I'll have to call Mary when we're cooking." He told Rose, "Will you let me do that... uninterrupted?" His eyes stared deeply into his sister's, and she smirked a bit.

"Jasper has a girlfriend! Jasper has a girlfriend!" Rose jokes, singing in a tune. Jasper's cheeks gain a red tint.

"Rose! You know that Mary is my best friend! Also, why are you hungry in the first place? Didn't your friend's mom drop you off and get you something beforehand?" Jasper asks, very annoyed and embarrassed. Rose shakes her head, and Jasper rolls his eyes.

"Ugh, you're so needy," he mumbled, then playfully grinned. I guess that this is what makes us siblings, though. Seriously, though, please let me talk to Mary, okay?"

"Fine, but my breakfast better be tasty," Rose giggled a bit, then skipped into the kitchen, where they both began to make the food. After several minutes, Jasper dialed Mary's number as he stirred the pot of Mac and Cheese. The phone rang until a tired voice answered.

"God, why so early?" Mary asked, yawning against the speaker of her phone.

"Sorry, I just saw your texts. What did you find about that magic show thing?" he asked, leaning back against the counter as Rose watched from a chair.

"Oh! Yeah, sorry, it took me a minute to remember. Yeah, I found out some pretty interesting history on it. Most websites are down that once had all the prior information on the place when it was still around, but you can access one website using the Wayback tool. You can find other facts easily, like what happened and stuff," she explained with another yawn. Rustling could be heard on the other end as she got out of bed.

"Well, don't leave me hanging on the details, Mary. You're making me all curious over here," Jasper turned his phone on speaker, leaning against the counter on his arms as the Mac and Cheese boiled in the water. Mary stretched her arms and legs as she walked around her room.

"Okay, so... I found out that this 'Papa Grande' guy has one helluva history with a theme park called 'West Virginia Dream Park,'" Mary told Jasper.

"They should have hired better people to name everything. That sounds so dumb," Jasper chuckled, then stirred the Mac and Cheese shells.

"Yeah, but that's not the important part. You see, Papa Grande's real name was Grande Alexander Willow, and he had been a magician at the theme park for well over thirty years. That's unbelievable, right? Well, in 1993, something happened with Grande," Mary's voice and the conversation caught Rose's attention.

"Okay, thirty years is insane. So what happened in 1993 that even my mother wanted to keep a secret?" Jasper asked while stirring the shells and checking to see if they were ready. Mary sighs softly.

"Well, to say that it was something small would be a lie. So, Grande Willow killed his boss, Richard, in 1993. It was his 30th performance anniversary, and he suddenly went into a rampage. He sawed his boss in half," Mary told Jasper, making him drop the wooden spoon into the boiling water in slight shock.

"Whoa, whoa, whoa, back up. That explains a hella lot. Was he ever caught?" he asks, trying to pick the spoon out of the water.

"Well, yes and no. It sounds like he escaped capture after being arrested, and it was like a wild goose chase or something. He ended up being considered dead after a few months of looking," Mary replied.

"What? You mean to tell me that the cops just backed off that quickly?" Jasper said. "I mean, for a guy to be considered dead that quickly, that's ridiculous..." Some noises echo in the background of the call as Mary moves stuff around in her room.

"It was the 90s. I'm sure that many things were going on. We're literally surrounded by mountains, think about it. Either way, it's 2014, not 1993. He is certainly dead by now or is in another state," Mary replied, calming Jasper down a bit.

"Yeah, that's true. Did you find anything else?" Jasper begins to finish the food, draining the water into the sink to add the cheese to the macaroni. Rose gets off of the chair and grabs a nearby bowl.

"Jasper, what if the guy went to a different state?" Rose asks, catching him off guard with the question. Mary begins to laugh.

"Oh? Is that Rose? Huh, so she's back from her friend's? You know, Rose, you shouldn't be listening to this conversation." Mary teases, causing Rose to groan.

"I'm eleven, not six! Also, Jasper put you on speakerphone; I can't just shut my ears off! Besides, I like this stuff too!" Rose pouts, looking at the phone. Mary and Jasper both laugh, finding amusement in her frustration, but she does get influenced by them.

"Okay, okay, you got us there." Jasper then filled Rose's bowl with mac and cheese.

"So, to answer your earlier question, yeah, I found more about this theme park." Mary continues, pulling up a web page on her end. "I found the location, actually. You can sort of see it on Google Maps. It looks pretty run down and is about a 35-minute walk from your house. So, are you thinking what I'm thinking?" Mary then closes her laptop. Jasper sighs and glances down at Rose, becoming a bit nervous.

"I don't know, Mary. Rose is with me, and you heard mom earlier; she would be so pissed."

"She is also at work right now; she won't know. Come on, could you imagine all the old merchandise and stuff in that place?" Mary said, convincingly. Jasper then feels Rose yank on his shirt, causing him to look down at her.

"Jasper, can we go? I want to see cool stuff!" Rose begs. "You never let me go exploring with you! I'm old enough now! Please!" Rose shakes him a bit. Jasper, feeling pressured, finally caved in.

"Fine, we can go, but we better not stay there long. Mom will legit skin me alive if I don't come home before she gets home." He then pointed his finger at Rose. "And you better stay near me, no games, got it?" Jasper demanded. Rose didn't exactly care for the lecture, but if it meant that she could come along for the trip, she would cooperate. With a quiet nod, Rose went to go and finish her food while Jasper ended the call with Mary. He was beginning to list off everything he would need to bring with him under his breath.

"I need my flashlight, bag, phone, maybe even my keys." He grabbed each one of the items as he traveled about his room, placing them into his bag. He didn't know how to feel in total since this would be the first time that Rose joined them in anything like this. Mary also seemed confident that everything would be okay. Placing his bag down, Jasper yawned and sprawled out against his bed. Some extra sleep would do him wonders; he was sure of it.

An hour had passed since Jasper fell asleep. As drool drained from his mouth, Rose's voice, followed by loud knocking, caused his eyes to crack open.

"Jasper, Mary's here!" Rose shouted, knocking again. Jasper's body rolled off the bed, and he gripped his backpack and threw it over his shoulder. For Mary to arrive so quickly certainly meant that she was excited about this adventure. Rose also sounded thrilled to be going along with them.

"Okay, okay, I'm up, hold on!" Jasper replied, exiting his room. Rose quickly darted down the stairs towards the front door where Mary was waiting. Mary flicked on a flashlight of her own and pointed it towards Jasper's face, causing him to recoil.

"Mary!" Jasper yelled, covering his eyes with his hand. Mary laughed, flicking it back off.

"Well, that's what you get for sleeping. I just had to make sure that you were awake! Any further complaints will be ignored!" Mary said with a smirk, reaching into her bag to put away the flashlight and grab a map. Jasper and Rose both glanced at the marked area on the sheet of paper. Jasper quickly assumed that was their destination, and Mary had planned this out pretty well. Though, a thought still struck a chord in Jasper's head, one that still made him feel on edge. Jasper knew that this was different than what they were used to.

"Are you sure that we should do this? All the other places we've gone to were just abandoned houses." Jasper said. Mary's expression started to grow more humored. It was evident that she found this wary side of Jasper amusing. What was he, a chicken?

"Ooh, are you scared that Richard's ghost will get you?" Mary said, taunting Jasper. Jasper's wary expression did not fade; it only became worse. Even Rose seemed less wary and continued to act excited.

"N-No, it's not that. I mean, you know what, never mind..." Jasper tried to explain, but neither of the girls would care. Through Mary's eyes, this was going to be just a typical abandoned place that was going to be skimmed through. The only scary thing in that place could be the mice infesting it. After all, the dead couldn't harm anyone.

"Come on, let's get going. The longer we hang around your house, the sooner your mom will get home." Mary gestures with her thumb towards the door. With a turn of the handle, both girls exit the house, leaving the unnerved Jasper trailing behind them.

The journey towards the abandoned theme park was more than a simple walk for them. They had to find many different routes to try and get there faster. Mary held the map the entire way, pointing at certain roads they could cross. After what felt like thirty minutes, they were finally close to their destination. The group slowed down to rest, placing their bags onto the grass in a large, open field. The field had a forest beside it, and several bushes and weeds were scattered. Jasper pulled out his phone and checked the time.

"Well, we should almost be there, right?" he asked, noticing Mary mark their steps on the map. She nodded and circled their current location. Her eyes moved over to stare at the large forest in the distance. That was enough of a hint for Jasper. She knew exactly where they were, and he could see the excitement grow on her face. Rose held her legs as she sat in the grass, seeming tired.

"Jasper, my legs hurt..." Rose tells her brother with a saddened expression.

"Well, you wanted to come with..." Jasper told her. He wasn't exactly wrong, and Rose grew annoyed; she knew he was right.

"We're almost there..." Mary assured suddenly, messing up Rose's hair as she stood back up. She then points at the forest. "There's our target, so who's ready to see this place? I know that I am!" She said, smiling at Jasper and Rose. Jasper sighed and stood up, stretching his legs a bit. Rose remained on the ground, not wanting to move.

"Come on, you two. The last one there will have to hold all the stuff that we find!" Mary yelled while walking through a couple of bushes. Jasper quickly bent down and picked Rose up onto his back. Rose sighed with relief as Jasper started to carry her.

"You know, I doubt we should take stuff from this place!" Jasper shouted, trying to catch up to Mary. Mary was not hesitating with her walking pace, nor was she going to answer him. Leaves crunched under their feet as they tramped deeper into the woods. It was tough to see, almost impossible, with all the vegetation surrounding them.

"Dang it, hey Rose, can you see anything?" Mary asked Rose. Being on Jasper's back, Rose observed the entire area and squinted her eyes. In the distance, something reflected some light at them, something tall. It was a fence covered in rusty patches and had several vines growing against it.

"Yeah, um... I think I see a fence," Rose replied to Mary. Mary lifted her arms in happiness. It was a relief to finally make it to their destination. After all, they typically never go this far to adventure into an abandoned place.

"We've finally made it! See, was that so bad?" Mary said while walking towards the fence, climbing over tree limbs and other debris that nature had left. Around the fence, several remnants of what used to exist remained sprawled about, like old sections of rusty signs, small segments of amusement park ride parts, and even some old bricks that used to be the parking lot.

"Can you see something?" Jasper asked, trying to move some vegetation aside to look through the fence. The sound of something climbing the fence catches (caught) him off guard. Mary had risen to the top.

"Jasper, you need to see this! Come on, this place is huge!" Mary said, while vaulting herself over the fence. This was it; this was the moment they were waiting for.

"Okay, I'm gonna send Rose over first!" Jasper called over to Mary and then placed Rose down. "You got this, okay? I'll be right behind you." Jasper told Rose, then patted her shoulder. Rose didn't look too amused but couldn't shake off being excited (her excitement). This was her first significant adventure, and even Jasper started to feel a bit excited about what truly awaited on the other side. With a grunt, Rose gripped the fence and began to climb. Jasper followed her below, and Mary waited with her arms open on the other side for Rose. The second Rose went over the top, she lost her grip and gasped in fear as she fell into Mary's arms. Mary grunted and nearly fell towards the fence.

"Whoa, is everything okay?!" Jasper asked, beginning to worry. "She better not have gotten hurt! I'd rather have my head when we get home!" He said, getting to the top of the fence. Rose was okay but was in Mary's arms, looking slightly embarrassed.

"I'm okay; I just lost my grip!" Rose admits, then gets out of Mary's arms. Jasper jumps down from the fence and landed on the ground. The group then brought their focus back to their surroundings, and it felt like they walked through a time machine. The building was way bigger than expected and had dull colors that were once vibrant. Windows that once stood tall were shattered like sharp knives with rain damage along the hinges. The doors, once plated with gold and steel, were now rusted, possibly to the point of being unable to open. The several vendor shops that once littered the theme park were broken down, but many necklaces remained on the table or the ground below, rusted and damaged to the point of being worthless to wear. The amusement park ride remnants had chipped paint and rust and had been broken down. Nature had indeed consumed most of this place, but that was the beauty of it for the trio, the mystery, and the remnants behind it. Mary didn't hesitate and immediately went towards the rusted doors to the building. Her hands grasped the handles, and she yanked, not feeling it budge. Around the building's lower windows, some wooden boards covered each of them, blocking anyone from entering the inside. It was evident that Mary was becoming frustrated compared to Jasper and Rose. Her face became scrunched up and agitated.

"Please tell me that this trip wasn't for nothing." She then kicked the door with her boot. Jasper's eyes trailed from the door to the boarded-up windows, then towards an old rusted chair nearby that sat against an old bush.

"Hold up; I have an idea. Back up and let me do something." Jasper told Mary while picking up the rusted chair. It felt slimy in his hands as she quickly swung it towards the boarded-up window. The window did not last and broke into many chunks, landing on the wooden flooring inside of the building. Jasper looked down at the chair or what remained, seeing that it was nothing but bent remains. Mary's eyes grew to become ecstatic.

"Awesome! Good thinking, Jasper! Though, wouldn't this count as property damage?" Mary said jokingly. Jasper rolled his eyes and then knocked the rest of the board away with his hand.

"Yeah, just don't tell mom..." Jasper then entered the building first, "Or anyone else."

It was incredibly dark in the building, with only the light from outside shining through the window. Wherever the light's rays hit, dust particles would move about, along with the overwhelming scent of interior decay mixed in.

"It smells gross here," Rose said while covering her nose. The mixture of rotten wood, moldy old clothes, and possible dead animals could cause even the more hardened soul to gag.

"Did you expect something abandoned since the nineties to smell like roses, Rose?" Mary nudged her arm against Rose.

"No, but I..." Rose is cut off by Jasper, who shined his light towards them.

"Hey, give Rose a break, Mary," Jasper said. "Also, what room is this even?" He then slowly trailed his flashlight around the room. Several articles of clothing were scattered about; most were overflowing from the closet that had broken hinges. In the center of the room was a bed and an old, rusty alarm clock.

"A hotel bedroom? I'm sure that this place was popular enough..." Mary murmured, then shined her light toward the many pictures on the wall. Each was covered with a layer of dust, blurring the images underneath. One image had a young boy and an older gentleman. The boy looked happy, while the older man seemed overjoyed in the photo while holding onto the boy's shoulders. Rose's expression grew saddened as she looked at this picture.

"What would it have been like today if nothing terrible had happened?"

Mary didn't know how to reply and pointed her flashlight towards the bedroom exit.

"Well, it's over now. Nothing will change what happened, but that's what makes exploring so cool. You get to discover more about a place, which allows you to imagine what could have been, you know?"

Jasper stepped forward and pointed his flashlight out of the room. "That, and sometimes, it's just the thrill of seeing something new," he added, then shined his flashlight around the long hallway. On one end, the hallway led into the lobby of the building, while on the other, it led towards the stairs that gave access to the stage area. Jasper's hand traveled towards his hip.

"Well, which way are we heading?" he asked. Rose pointed her finger towards the stairs. Jasper and Mary both shined their lights in that direction.

"Alright, guess we'll go that way. After all, we could go the other way on the way out to leave," Jasper said while softly nudging Rose. Rose nudged him back as the floorboards creaked under their feet.

A soft, dripping noise echoed the closer they got to the stairs. Stepping through the door, he noticed that the staircase in front of them seemed slightly damaged, with several chunks of wood missing along with a segment of missing railing. Mary shined her light upwards as something wet landed on her head.

"Huh, what's that?" she asked Jasper and Rose. Rose squinted her eyes to see. Above them, a tall tank half full of water had been knocked against the railing and was leaking badly.

"I guess that we should be careful; that thing seems about ready to fall..." Jasper then pointed his light toward the floor, where glass shards reflected light back towards him. "Also, there's glass. I'd rather not have to go to the hospital today." He sighed, taking his first step up the stairs. Rose and Mary both stepped around the glass. Each step up the stairs made unsettling noises, almost like they could snap under their feet if given enough pressure. They carefully went up one at a time until they could see the water from the tank reflect back the light from their flashlights.

Across from the tank, a thick wooden door stood tall with its hinges intact. Much of the paint that once existed on it seemed faded, lost to time, much like many things the building once offered. However, the handle on the door was the most worn and even looked slightly busted and stained with rust. Rose gripped the handle and turned it, yet it seemed jammed.

"Jasper, it's stuck..."

"Here, let me try," Jasper's hand gripped the handle next. He twisted it hard, and thankfully, it didn't break. The door creaked slowly open, allowing light to appear from the room on the other side. Jasper carefully looked into the room, and his eyes went wide. He gagged suddenly and covered his nose.

"Jesus, it smells like pure garbage in there!" Jasper yelled. Mary softly slapped his back, giving him an annoyed look. Jasper was right, though. The trio entered the room, and each one covered their noses. It did smell horrendous, like an animal had passed away while being baked under the sun for several hours.

The room itself was none other than the stage room. The stage was in the center, and various antique seats lined the room. The stage that once had beautiful red curtains now had faded pink ones, each torn at the base and destroyed near the top. The several stained glass windows around the room were more damaged than they looked outside, with their borders decayed and damaged. The wooden floors also had several missing segments, and the center of the stage had a brown stain, one that seeped into the wood to become permanent. Jasper's blood ran cold at the sight, and his throat tightened.

"This is so messed up," Jasper admitted. "Is that Richard's blood?" Mary grabbed Jasper's arm.

"There is only one way to find out," Mary replied. Jasper tried to tug away.

"Mary, are you kidding me?!" Jasper said, shocked that she would even want to get a closer look.

Feeling disgusted by the room's smell and Mary's curiosity, Rose stepped towards the window for some fresh air. The breeze caught her hair, and she looked around. Several squirrels ran about the fenced-in area of the building, one even running through an open part of the fence that they must have missed on the way in. She leaned against the window, feeling tired from traveling. Behind her, Jasper and Mary bickered.

"I don't want to get closer!" Jasper yelled, being pushed by Mary onto the stage.

"It's interesting!" Mary huffed.

"No, it's-" Jasper then stumbled forward and landed on the last step of the stage with a thud, causing the step to snap.

Rose's eyes darted toward Jasper, and after Jasper rubbed his now sore ankle with little injury, her attention was drawn back outside. Trees shifted in the breeze, and shadows moved, yet something felt off. Out of the corner of her eye, something moved. It was not the shadow of a squirrel; it was taller and human. Her eyes widen, and she turns her head to look at Jasper and Mary.

"G... Guys, something-" Rose gets interrupted by Jasper, who holds his ankle.

"Damn it, that hurt! I need to sit down for a minute," Jasper gritted his teeth and then glared at Mary. Mary keeps her gaze towards him, seemingly a bit worried about him. Rose's eyes quickly moved to look at the mysterious shadow again, but it was gone; it had vanished.

Rose's heart started to race quickly in her chest. Jasper rubbed his ankle, and Mary faced away from Jasper with a frown on her face. Her eyes then locked onto another door towards the right of the stage area.

"Since you need to rest, I'll explore a bit more. Stay off that foot. I'm sorry for pushing you," Mary apologized, touching Jasper's shoulder.

"Yeah, yeah, go ahead. I'll be okay," Jasper assured, then glanced back at the old brown splotches around the stage. Rose walked up to Jasper with her arms tucked close to her. Her eyes nervously dashed from the window to Jasper and back again. Her throat felt tighter, and her paranoia grew higher.

"J-Jasper, can we go home now?" Rose asked, watching as Mary walked into the room not far ahead of them. Jasper raised his eyebrow and frowned.

"Are you okay? What's up with the sudden attitude change?" Jasper asked, noticing her demeanor. Rose started to stutter.

"I-I-I..."

"Rose, we'll be leaving soon, don't worry," Jasper said, touching her shoulder. This did not assure her one bit.

Mary, meanwhile, opened the door to another room and was busy exploring the inside of a large bedroom. The bedroom seemed much like the one downstairs, but it was in better condition, with various items neatly placed on the bed, dresser, and floor. A photo of a man and a woman on the dresser piqued her curiosity.

"Hey, Jasper-" She hesitated; Jasper still rested his ankle in the other room.

"Who are you...?" She tilted her head slightly at the picture, then lifted it to try and read the back. The writing seemed faded, as did the corners of the image. The woman had short black hair, and the man was none other than Grande himself.

"My dearest love...?" she mouthed, barely able to read the writing. Suddenly, a soft ping caught her attention, and she placed the photo back down. Near her feet, a necklace was sprawled on the floor; it had to have fallen from the photo frame.

"Mary, are you done inside of there?! Rose is beginning to-" Jasper quickly gets cut off by his sister.

"I swear, Jasper! I saw something! I wanna go home!" Rose cried. The yelling slightly destroyed Mary's focus, but her thoughts were rushing. Her hand moved in, then she gripped the necklace between her fingers, feeling the peridot gem in the center. It was beautiful as if she was looking at a wide valley.

"I'm done! It's just a bedroom, nothing too special!" Mary lied, then neatly stuffed the necklace into her pocket so she could have a souvenir. A part of her felt as if she'd get in genuine trouble if she showed anyone, but at the same time, who could miss something abandoned for years?

Mary exited the room and closed the door behind her. Jasper and Rose were both still talking to one another.

"Rose, it could have been an animal," Jasper stared into her eyes. Stomping her foot, she shook her head and pushed him a bit.

"No! It was a person! I'm sure it was a person!" Rose yelled, 'It was a tall shadow, Jasper! This always happens in horror movies!" Rose said, beginning to panic. Jasper shook his head and moved to stand up.

"Okay, if you are that worried, we can leave now. It's getting close to mom getting home anyway," Jasper placed his hand on Rose's head and messed up her hair. Rose didn't seem amused and kept her head on a swivel as she walked close to Jasper.

Mary glanced back at the bedroom one last time, then felt the necklace in her pocket between her fingers again. A part of her wanted to put it back, yet this was something special, something unique. She kept ahold of it as they left the room. Jasper used his flashlight to view his surroundings as they moved down the stairs. Jasper nearly stumbled down them as his ankle coursed pain up his body.

"Ow..." He winced, then gripped the small amount of railing that was left. Mary frowned.

"You might have sprained or twisted something," she said, holding onto Jasper to keep him somewhat steady.

"You think?" Jasper murmured, and then a loud crack echoed around the room as Jasper's shoe landed on the glass shards from before. Hearing such a noise, Rose emitted a shriek of fear and quickly ran out of the room. Jasper and Mary both gasped, not expecting Rose to run off.

"Rose!" they yelled, then quickly rushed to try to follow her. Jasper flinched and gasped as his ankle grew more painful with each step, and seconds later, he had to stop and press himself against the wall.

"Mary, get Rose. My ankle is killing me," Jasper said, taking a minute to rest.

"Why did she run off like that?" Mary asked herself, quickly trying to follow Rose.

Rose didn't stop running, not even for a second. The dark halls of the building wrapped her body in an eerie embrace. Her fight or flight mode ran rampant as her legs carried her with little thought on where she was heading. She had to hide; she just had to. She moved her hands along the wall and finally felt a door handle. With a sharp twist, the door slid open, and she ran into the room, closing the door behind her. It was pitch black inside, and Mary's voice could faintly be heard down the hall. Rose felt around with her hands still stretched out. She bumped into many objects in her way and felt a cloth of some sort. She ran her fingers along it and quickly went under it, curling herself into the corner of the room with it over her body. If she could not see, the thing she saw could not see; that was what any child would think. Mary's voice echoed, "Rose?! Where did you go!?"

At first, Rose wanted to call out for her and answer her, but then she heard a sound, one far too close to her for comfort. Thud, thud, thud. Rose gripped the cloth sheet tightly over herself, curling against herself tighter and tighter. She feared the worst, yet silence quickly arrived, and the thudding stopped. She felt a moment of relief; maybe it was her heart pounding in her ears. She slowly lowered the cloth that was over her body and looked forward. Her eyes were beginning to see better in the dark, and the outline of several pieces of old furniture made her skin crawl. She kept quiet, then kept glancing around to make sure the coast was clear. Perhaps she had acted upon her own fear too quickly; maybe Jasper and Mary were both right.

Mary's quick footsteps and flashlight shined through the bottom of the door, surprising Rose.

"Rose? Are you around here? I know that I saw you run this way!" Mary asked. Rose went to grab the door handle, but before she could, a loud noise echoed down the hall, making her entire body freeze in fear. Mary's flashlight pointed away, and the room went dark again.

"Rose, are you leaving the building? Get over here before you hurt yourself!" Mary shouted, then walked away from the door. Rose's eyes grew horrified, and she gripped the door handle. She wanted to yell out to Mary, but her mouth remained closed from fear. Her hand trembled, and then she opened the door and looked around through the crack she made.

Mary stood near the door to the room where they first entered the building. She had a puzzled look on her face.

"You know, if you were scared that someone was outside, you shouldn't leave the building," Mary said. "Stop playing around and stay by us, okay? I know that you're freaked out, but this is ridiculous." Mary pushed the door part way open and shined her flashlight forward. One of the old closet doors blocked the window they entered through as if it had fallen over. Rose opened the door fully, and Mary quickly turned to face her.

"Rose?"

Rose had a guilty expression on her face.

"I'm sorry, Mary..." Rose apologized, almost in tears. Mary lowered her flashlight slightly.

"You didn't have to close the window up, you know? Everything's okay," Mary said, placing a hand on her hip. Rose quickly became confused.

"M... Mary, I didn't close the window up. I was only in this room," Rose replied while touching the handle. Mary's gaze moved from Rose to the direction of the blocked window.

"Then..." Mary's flashlight moved around the room again, but this time, something white slowly landed in the distance of the open doorway. It was a flower petal. Rose and Mary both went still.

A flower petal that appeared so delicate made them become paralyzed with anxiety. Mary's hand started to shake as the flower petal remained near the open door. The flashlight illuminated further up until one thing stuck out. Against the door, holding it, a gray gloved hand made itself known. Mary's mouth went dry, and she kept her flashlight pointed at it.

"G... Get behind me," she whispered sternly, then backed up cautiously, pulling Rose behind her. The younger girl didn't hesitate and stood behind Mary. Rose was right; they, indeed, were not alone. The further they backed up, the more the person in the room opened the door to make themselves visible. Brown, bloodshot eyes locked onto them, eventually followed by the sound of a grunt as the figure stepped into view. It was a man and not a young one. He had gray, medium-length hair, a dirty tank top, and some muscle underneath. An unkempt beard on his face blended with his facial scars; in his other hand, he had a bouquet of dead flowers. He stood in the doorway, staring at them both with an agitated expression. He released the flowers from his grip, allowing them to join the singular petal on the hardwood floor. He was creepily silent, not letting his gaze leave them for even a second. Mary continued backing away slowly, keeping the light directly against him. Rose's eyes dripped with tears—she was right.

"W-Who are you?" Rose asked, breaking the silence and tension between everyone. The man didn't respond right away and stepped into the hall, slowly beginning to follow them with his eyes unmoving from them both. Mary gripped her flashlight tightly and was beginning to feel her fight or flight kick in.

"R-Rose, be quiet," she whispered.

His eyes slowly focused on Rose.

"Who... am I?" His voice sounded strained, and his teeth were clenched together. "T... That does not matter. Why are you here? Why, why?!" the man asked angrily, causing the girls to tense up even more.

"We were just about to leave-" Mary trembled, and Rose felt that urge to run strike her once again.

"All of you are the same. You break in, you try to take; that's all everyone has done to me! Take, take, take!" he yelled, clenching his fists. "What did you do? Hm? Why are you here?!" He asked again, this time more aggressively, as he took one step towards them with his eyebrows scrunched together.

"W-We didn't take anything!" Mary yelled, glancing in every direction. Both girls knew that something wasn't right. There wasn't a police badge on this man. Rose tugged on Mary's pants, and a ping echoed in the hall as she did. Underneath Mary, the peridot necklace from before was once again sprawled out on the floor. The girls went deathly silent, as did the man in the hallway with them. It was quiet as their eyes remained locked on one another, but the man took notice, and his knuckles turned white as he did.

"That necklace, you tried to take it…?" he asked, his lips started to spasm. "You…" he trailed off, then emitted a scream of rage. Before the girls could react, the man dashed at Mary and slammed his shoulder against her. Her body slammed against the nearby wall, knocking over a flower vase in the collision.

"Mary!" Rose yelled, watching as the flashlight rolled across the floor. The man quickly bent down and pulled (picked up) the necklace off (from) the floor as Mary writhed in pain. The vase had smashed under her, and her arm was covered in cuts, and some parts even had segments even lodged into her flesh.

"R-Rose, run," she told her, "Go to Jasper, now!" She glared at the man and grasped a section of the broken vase in her hand. Rose listened and started running in the opposite direction, leaving Mary behind. Mary slowly got up to her feet, watching the man keep his eyes on the necklace. His lip trembled, and his body tensed up as tears developed in his eyes.

Mary quickly moved forward with her arm raised, the sharp section of the vase gripped tightly in her hand. To her sheer horror, his hand grabbed her wrist tightly, stopping her before she could stab him. Her eyes stared into his own as a tear dripped down his cheek.

"You have not a single clue about what you've done!" He snapped, then tossed Mary against the floor. She rolled and gasped in pain, then stood up quickly to start running away from the man. He stood there, glaring her down with a dark, enraged expression.

"Run, rabbit," he hissed, beginning to follow her at a relatively fast pace. Rose's soft sobbing could be heard where Jasper was left waiting for the duo to return. Mary felt some relief but held her arm as she bumped into various objects, unable to see because of the loss of her flashlight.

"Jasper!" she yelled, feeling as the blood from her cuts trickled down her arm. She could see Jasper's flashlight in the distance, much to her relief. Her expression relaxed somewhat, but overall, her heart was racing. As she entered the stairway, she gripped the door and closed it tightly. Rose's tears soaked into Jasper's clothes as she hid behind him. The older brother was obviously confused, and nobody explained the situation. His brows were raised, and his lips parted in shock.

"Mary, are you bleeding-"

"Jasper, Rose was right! We're in deep shit!" she interrupted and placed her back against the door. He emitted a frustrated sigh.

"Can someone explain what the hell is going on?!"

Rose hiccuped and tugged at his shirt.

"There's a scary man! He's out there! He hurt Mary!" she sobbed. Jasper's eyes widened in shock, and he quickly understood.

"Okay, let me call for help," Jasper sighed, digging into his bag for his phone.

"Little rabbit!" the man's voice echoed in the hallway right outside the door. Mary's eyes squeezed shut as she pressed her body against the door.

"Hurry, Jasper!" she begged. Jasper's eyes narrowed slightly in disbelief as he struggled to find his phone.

"Uh oh..." Jasper whispered. Mary shook her head quickly.

"No, no, no! Oh, come on, damn it, Jasper!" she yelled, then heard the handle beginning to turn next to her head. She gripped it and used her body to try and hold the door shut. A loud bang echoed outside, and the door jolted open for a second, revealing the man's angry eyes.

"Let me in! You stupid brat!" he screamed over and over, continuing to slam against the door.

"Rose, run!" Jasper yelled to his sister, pushing her up the stairs. With a quick limp forward, he also pressed his back against the door and held his breath, feeling the man's angered shoves continue to press against it. Mary's eyes dripped with tears, and she bit her lip, pushing hard to try and keep the door shut.

"I can't do this much longer!" Mary cried while sliding down the door. Jasper quickly looked around as the flashlight lit the room, and he could see the reflection of the glass shards on the floor. His gaze moved back and forth between the scene and the glass.

"Mary, run!" he said, forming an idea inside his head. Mary gasped, her eyes narrowing in disbelief.

"What?! You can't take this guy alone! Your foot-" Mary didn't get to finish her sentence as Jasper pushed her away from the door.

"Go!" he yelled again, his back pressed against the door even harder. The older man stopped for a second, but his angry grunts turned into the sound of sprinting.

"Oh shi-" The door slammed open, knocking Jasper back against the floor. The older man was standing above him, his brown eyes seeming to glow with a type of ferocity seen in a serial killer. Drool dripped from his lips as his eyes locked onto the teens.

"You disrespectful little shit!" the man screamed. "You come into my building and disrespect me?!" he continued to yell, wrapping his hands around Jasper's throat. The young man started to gag; it felt as if his throat was being torn apart. Mary didn't hesitate and quickly grabbed the glass shards from the ground, cutting into her hand in return.

"Hey, asshole!" she yelled and slammed the glass shards against the man's face. He screeched in pain. Each small segment of glass felt like a thousand daggers, leading him to lean against the wall with his mouth wide open.

Mary winced and held her hand. The young teen had pushed her luck, so the older man had finally entirely lost it. He began cursing loudly and jerked around.

"You little shit! My face! I'll kill you!" he started to grip his face as the teen duo quickly made their way up the stairs. With the door slammed shut, Jasper promptly looked around and grabbed an old seat from the stage area, shoving it under the handle with force. They both backed away and took time to breathe.

Rose was tucked underneath the curtains near the windows. Her jaw trembled as tears trailed down her cheeks.

"W... We're gonna die, aren't we?" she asked. Jasper shook his head quickly and limped over to his sister.

"Don't say that, we're gonna be okay," he whispered to her. Mary continued looking around for a way out. She dashed over towards the stage and climbed up onto it. The smell of rot only intensified as she approached the back of the stage.

"Maybe there's an exit this way?!" she asked the brother and sister duo. Jasper's eyebrows lowered a bit.

"How should I know?! Go and look! I'm occupied right now!" he snapped, holding his sister close as she sobbed. "It's okay, Rose, it's okay."

Mary threw her arms in the air and angrily pulled the curtains back from the stage. The velvet curtains moved to the side, and to her horror, the door was boarded shut and locked tight. Her mouth dropped, and her hands started to shake.

"T-There's... no way out," she said, bringing a hand through her hair to grip her head. Jasper stood up, still holding his sister close to his side.

"You've got to be kidding me!" he yelled. Mary went quiet, and tears started falling down her cheeks. Her breathing even started to increase in pace.

"W-Why did you take it?" Rose suddenly spoke up, breaking the silence. Mary's silence filled the room with more tension. Jasper's gaze turned harsh.

"Mary, what did you do?" he muttered between clenched teeth. Mary didn't know how to respond and felt her hands twitch. Her gaze could not meet his own, not even for a second. His expression only darkened more. "Mary, don't ignore me! What did you do?!"

"Just shut up! We have more to worry about than some dumb necklace I took!" she snapped back, hopping down from the stage. Jasper closed his eyes trying to calm down.

Before they could say anything else, loud footsteps echoed from behind the closed door, followed by the door handle being rattled and kicked. The chair jolted with each kick.

"He's up," Jasper whispered shakily, then looked over towards the window. Mary looked as well and rushed over towards it.

"What are you doing?!" he limped towards her. Rose kept her grip on her older brother and flinched at each kick against the door. She glared at him. "What choice do we have?! I won't just stand here and let some freak get us!" She then stepped out of the window and onto the roof. Jasper felt his stomach turn, but Mary did have a point. He didn't want to argue anymore. He pushed Rose ahead of him and climbed out onto the roof. The roof had various tiles missing and had ivy growing all over the side. Rose tucked close to Mary.

A loud slam echoed through the room as the door slammed open. Footsteps echoed through the room, and the man mumbled to himself in a low voice.

"You cannot hide forever," he hissed. "The audience wishes to see you. Everyone gets a bit of stage fright," he suddenly said, pulling back the stage curtains.

Jasper's eyes narrowed, and confusion filled his head. What audience? The room was empty. The man dragged his hand through his gray hair. His face was covered in blood from the glass shards. He was grinning as if growing manic.

"Please, come out. Don't be afraid. I'm choosing you to be my volunteer. That's why you came in here; that's why you broke in! You came to see me, the great Papa Grande Di Magico!" he laughed while slamming the door shut, locking their only other escape route. Jasper's grip on the ivy tightened, and sweat trailed down his forehead. Realization finally dawned on him as it did for everyone else. This sick man was none other than the magician that the adults in the area tried desperately to forget, Grande Alexander Willow.

Grande only grew angrier the longer he couldn't find them, dragging him further into his psychotic mindset. He was talking to no one on the outside, but on the inside, 'they' wouldn't stop talking to him. He gripped his hair tightly.

"Shut up! Shut up!" He yelled. "You damn kids are making the audience very angry! Where are you?!" The trio didn't know what to do or even think. Out of the corner of Jasper's eye, he saw Mary start to sway, her body drifting from side to side. Her grip on the ivy tightened, but she was beginning to lose focus. Blood trailed down her arm from the piece of vase shard lodged in her flesh.

"M-Mary?" Rose whispered. Jasper quickly held out his free hand, and his heart started to race even faster. Mary stumbled a bit, causing Grande's eyes to snap in their direction.

"There you are!" He yelled and dashed towards the window. Mary's eyes closed partway, and she gasped in horror as Grande managed to grab her ankles. She tumbled onto her knees, and Rose, to her brother's horror, started to slip down the roof.

"Jasper!" Rose screamed, gripping a few tiles as she desperately tried to hold on. The teenage girl didn't hesitate and gritted her teeth.

"Let me go!" she hissed and, with the last of her strength, kicked Grande away from her. Jasper lunged forward to try and grab his sister, but to his dismay, his fingers missed her shirt by a few centimeters. His eyebrows arched, and his mouth opened without allowing a single breath of air into his lungs. She was going to fall, and he felt helpless. He kept his hand stretched out, but before the little girl could fall off, Mary pushed herself forward and grabbed her hand.

"I got you..." she whispered to Rose weakly. Her eyes struggled to stay open as she pulled Rose up and weakly pushed her towards her brother. Jasper gripped Rose tightly and held her close, almost breaking into tears.

"A... Are you okay?" he asked her. Rose sniffled and buried her face against him. Mary tried to stand, but a snap echoed under her as she put all her weight onto the roof. The world seemed to freeze around them at that moment. Before she could take another step, the roof gave out from under her.

"No! Grab onto me!" Jasper screamed. He moved his hand out to grab her, but it was far too late. He stood there in disbelief as Mary's fingers grasped the gutter. Their eyes locked together one last time, and then a snap echoed through the air. She faded from sight as gravity gripped her body. Then, there was a loud, bone-breaking thud, followed by silence.

The world went still for the surviving teen and child. Grande's laughter echoed, and Jasper's brows furrowed, his hands balled into fists. Rose gripped the ivy, shaking her head at her brother's shift in temper.

"You bastard!" Jasper yelled, then went back into the room. Grande's eyes widened with glee.

"Ah! Is that the way to speak to your boss?" He asked, beginning to breathe deeply. "What's wrong? I thought that she was levitating. The audience was more than pleased!" The older man smirked. Jasper wasn't thinking clearly, not anymore. He gritted his teeth and picked up the earlier chair off the ground.

"You demented son of a bitch!" He yelled, then suddenly swung the chair towards Grande. Grande laughed loudly as the chair smashed across his back. He felt the pain somewhat, yet his adrenaline was far too high to react.

"No worries. I can tell you have stage fright. Let me help you!" Grande gripped a piece of the now broken chair, and with a swift, anger-fueled move, Grande slammed the remaining chair across Jasper's head, knocking him out cold.

Rose watched with her hand over her mouth as Jasper's unconscious body started to get dragged by Grande toward the stage.

"No! Let him go!" Rose screamed suddenly, climbing back into the room. She ran towards Jasper and gripped his jacket sleeve. "Let him go! Let him go!" She cried. Grande smirked.

"Oh, child, I will let him go once I perform. Tell me, do you like magic?" He asked Rose, his brown eyes gleaming with mixed emotions, including excitement. Rose sniffled and shook her head.

"Ah, I see... such a shame."

Grande didn't stop tugging Jasper until Rose finally lost her grip. The room was beginning to feel smaller for her. She moved towards the corner of the room and sat in a ball, horrified. She could not do anything but watch as the curtains were lowered and Grande disappeared with her brother. After nearly an hour of silence, it was beginning to get dark outside. Jasper's eyelids twitched, and he groaned. His head throbbed with pain, and his eyes grew dry and sore.

"Leave Rose alone," he whispered, trying to move, yet he couldn't. "Rose, run," he begged, trying to see his surroundings, yet all he could see was darkness. His nostrils twitched as a foul scent entered his nose. The scent reeked of decay, stronger than it had ever been. He tried to move once more, but this time, he could feel that he was inside something rectangular, a box of some sort.

"Ah, you're finally awake. I was beginning to worry," Grande said, flicking on a light to illuminate the surrounding area. Jasper's eyes adjusted, and as they did, he came face to face with the older man, who was wearing a magician's outfit with a top hat. His outfit was stained with old blood, but it did not faze him. "You cooperated quite well, and you even have a… guest waiting for you to perform. It is such a good feeling, being adored and treated like a star," he whispered while patting the large box the teen was locked into.

Jasper's voice cracked.

"Rose? You better leave her alone!" he snapped, kicking around inside the box. Grande laughed softly.

"Children only wish to see a show, not perform in them, you stupid boy," he replied, then gripped the table Jasper was on top of. Jasper breathed quickly.

"Why are you doing this?! It's not our fault that your life was ruined!" he said suddenly. Grande paused, and his voice went low and stern.

"Don't act like you understand me, you brat. You don't know anything! Now, shut your mouth! You will not stall me any longer!" Grande snapped, continuing to push the table Jasper was on. Jasper continued to yell, thrashing around inside the box.

"You killed your boss! He was innocent! We're innocent!" he yelled. Grande gritted his teeth together, and with a hard shove, the table rolled with Jasper against the stained stage curtains.

"He was not innocent! He took everything that I had left from me! I begged him to have mercy, yet he did not falter! Now, shut your damn mouth, you little shit!" He gripped his top hat, trying to compose himself. Grande's emotions were running wild, and the voices in his head only grew stronger. It was his time to shine as the magician, and the audience cheered him on. A faint smile grew on his stressed-out face.

"Can you hear them? Hm?" he asked Jasper. "They are all outside, waiting for us to perform! You are my actor, my volunteer. We'll make them all amazed." Grande chuckled deeply.

"I-I don't hear-" Jasper couldn't speak any longer as Grande pulled the curtains open, and Jasper's mouth dropped. The scent of decay was enough to make him want to vomit, but the sight in front of him made his stomach fully twist.

Chairs were stacked in the room, all organized and neat. On the chairs, multiple corpses were in different positions, all having different expressions on their decomposing faces. Some were twisted in horror and had their flesh eaten by several maggot larvae. Some corpses even had wounds on their bodies, and one even had a missing lower half. In the corner of the room, Rose was curled up in a ball, staring off into the distance, her eyes bloodshot from crying.

"J-Jasper..." Her voice was but a whisper; she was entirely in shock.

Jasper rapidly kicked at the bottom of the box, and Grande stepped ahead, clearing his throat.

"Greetings, my lovely audience! It is I, Papa Grande Di Magico! Today, we have an extraordinary show and an exceptional guest! This young man bravely volunteered himself to be our new actor for today! Please, give him a round of applause!" Grande stretched his arms out with a bow. In his head, he could hear the claps of the crowd, the cheers, the carnival music, everything. In reality, the corpses sat silent, with only the sniffling from Rose making any noise.

Grande straightened himself and grinned, "I'm glad to hear your excitement today!" He laughed happily, then walked towards the back room. "I have an extraordinary trick to show you today, my audience! Allow me to give you a hint!" He then disappeared into the back area. Jasper's eyes remained unaltered towards Rose; she was physically unharmed, much to his relief.

"R-Rose!" He called out, "Rose, hide! Rose!" Jasper begged, yet she did not budge. She only whispered under her breath and looked rattled. The magician quickly returned, holding a large, rusty hacksaw that had grown slightly damaged due to past use. Jasper grew extremely desperate; his voice became strained.

"Now, my lovely audience, please give a round of applause to my special volunteer as we perform my favorite trick! The Half Man! It has been so many weeks since I have performed for you all, and now, watch as I deliver a magical performance!" Grande announced with a loud and confident voice. He lifted the saw, positioning the sharp edges along the wooden box that the teen was trapped in.

"Help me!" Jasper thrashed his head left and right, kicking his feet against the bottom of the box. "I-I'm going to die! I didn't do anything to you! I didn't do-"

The loud echo of a slap followed by searing pain quickly silenced Jasper. Grande's face turned red, "Don't interrupt me! It's insulting!" He yelled. Grande then adjusted his top hat and grasped the hacksaw handle, beginning to move the sharp blade back and forth against the box. Wood shavings fell, landing as softly as a feather against the stage floor. Jasper felt at a loss and closed his eyes tightly.

"Now, here is the finale!" Grande's sawing became faster, with every movement causing Jasper's entire body to tense up until his screams of pain filled the whole room. The sound of mashing flesh and bones being cut into echoed wall to wall. The teen threw his head back as his eyes rolled into his skull. He could not move as his spine cracked and snapped in half. His hands trembled as his nerves become damaged from the movement of the hacksaw.

"You're doing very well!" Grande laughed as his shoes stepped directly into the formed blood puddle below. Jasper did not reply nor move as Grande finally forced the hacksaw through him entirely. The hacksaw landed on the floor with a ping. Grande's gloved hands grasped the box and grinned at the "audience." Rose's face was soaked in tears once again, and she finally emitted a loud, blood-curdling scream as the two halves of the box were separated, allowing the guts of the teen to fall out part by part onto the floor. Grande's hand gripped the rim of his hat, and he turned to the "audience" and bowed.

"Thank you all for joining me today, and give a round of applause to my wonderful actor," he said, gesturing over towards Jasper's corpse as if he was still alive as well. His attention then fell onto Rose.

"Little girl, did you enjoy the show?" Grande asked, beginning to step off of the stage.

"You killed him!" Rose screamed, "You killed him!" she repeated, grasping the handle of the door. She wanted to leave; she wanted to be free of this nightmare.

The magician's entire body suddenly stopped moving.

"What?! He is very much alive!" he said, agitated. The child cried louder and yanked at the door.

"You killed him!" she kept repeating, but this time, the old magician turned to look at the various seats and Jasper. A gasp escaped his lips as the hallucinations started to fade, revealing what he had done once again to another set of innocent lives. His eyes traveled to his soaked gloves and magician attire. His hands started to shake violently, and his face became strained as if he were trying to hold back a scream of his own. He slowly moved his hand into his pocket and shakily unlocked the door.

"G-Get out of here, you brat."

Rose quickly stood up and stumbled out the door, sprinting out of the room without hesitation. The older man stood silently, looking over the mess he had caused. His fingers went through his hair, and finally, a loud and emotional scream echoed through the entire building as his emotional and physical pain set in.

Rose could hear the scream as she stumbled through the dark. Items fell around her as she slammed into them, disoriented and scared. Her exit was near; she was released, but why? Her heart raced inside her chest as she saw the blocked window shine with an opening big enough for her to slip through. There was her exit, her chance at freedom. She squeezed past everything and finally made it outside. She landed on the ground with a thud and quickly started to sprint over toward the open segment of the fence. Out of the corner of her eye, Mary's body was sprawled on the ground. Rose's eyes widened as Mary's hand started to twitch.

"R-Rose, help me," she spoke weakly. Rose hesitated, being far too afraid to do anything. Mary weakly stretched out her arm, but it lowered as her eyes finally closed.

"Run," Mary whispered hoarsely, going limp against the ground. With the turn of her heel, Rose sprinted out of the surrounding area of the building. She was free from the nightmare, yet not free from her fear. As she stumbled through weeds and bushes, she felt thorns stick to her and branches trip her. She grunted and swiped at various bugs that flew around her head. Tears fogged her vision as she kept sprinting. She was not looking back for even a second.

"Mommy! Mommy!" she yelled, finally seeing the edge of the forest in her view. The welcoming light reached out for her with open arms. She was free, away from the madness.

SNAP!

Pain shot through her leg as she fell roughly into a steep ditch. Her emotions finally poured out as she curled into herself. Her leg ached, and her foot felt twisted.

"J-Jasper, M-Mary…" she sobbed. That would be the last time she would see her sibling, friend, and mom. The child remained sprawled out in the woods, lost, cold, and afraid. Drawn in by curiosity and a knack for exploring, an adventure once thought to be fun had turned disastrous. None of the three kids ever returned home. This was their end, their true, horrible finale.

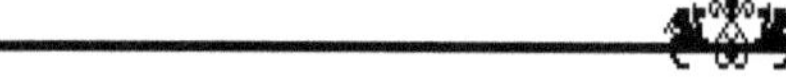